M000288438

FROM THE HEART OF

GOD

WHAT DOES GOD SAY?

Mrs. Sadie Stokes - Thompkins

Copyright © 2021 Sadie Stokes- Thompkins.
All rights reserved.

No portion of this book may be reproduced mechanically, electronically, or by any other means, including photocopying, without the author's written permission. It is illegal to copy this book, post it on a website, or distribute it by any other means without permission from the author.

Pataskity Publishing Co.

207 Hudson Trce Suite 102

Augusta, GA 30907

(706) 250-3956

www.pataskitypublishing.com

ISBN: 978-1-948605-37-3

CONTENTS

DEDICATIONS

I dedicate this book to my grandmother, **Susie Wright**
who raised me and has gone home to the Lord.

DEDICATIONS

I dedicate this book to my loving husband, Ira Thompkins.
Thank you for always being my listening ear!

DEDICATIONS

I dedicate this book to my daughter, **Arteasia**.

Arteasia (TEASY/SKEETER)

You were born out of love, and Heavenly sent from up above.

You are my inspiration encouraging me to face the nation.

I have been down, but you lifted me up.

You, not even knowing that you lightened my cup.

I am so proud of the beautiful woman you have become

Jumping over hurdles or knocking them down one by one.

I am especially proud of you for being yourself!

You are understanding, and compassionate.

You always do good for those in need of help.

You are the best daughter any mother could ever have!

We have had our share of ups and downs,

But thank God for our many laughs.

I have seen your hurt and pain.

Through it all, God kept you in his hands.

Your mother is here with all that she's got.

It may seem little but coming from the heart it is a lot!

DEDICATIONS

———o———

Malik Wright

I dedicate this book to my son whom I love so much, **Malik Wright**. My prayer is that God's hand will give you a special touch. You are a humble child. I must admit you stay to yourself. I was working hard on two jobs when with you is where my time should have been spent. I cannot change the past. I can only look to the future. Please listen to God, and not to a bunch of confusion. God loves you! He entrusted you to me. I only want you to be closer to Jesus because he is the only one who can set you free. I have been there, done that. I have felt what you are feeling. But all the mess, Satan threw at me, you do not have to play what he is dealing Satan in hell. He is moving really swift. Can't you tell? Just look around at the world today. Read from Genesis to Revelation. God's word is here to stay. All of the things that happened back then have come back around because we have turned from God to a world of sin. My unconditional love is crying out for the human soul. To God be the glory for it is him who you have chosen.

I not only dedicate this book to my children, but also to my grandchildren and great grandchildren. I love each of you!

ACKNOWLEDGEMENTS

This book is also dedicated to my Uncle **Henry Stokes** who constantly encouraged me to publish my poems.

To my cousin, **Franklin Stokes**. Thank you for never ceasing to encourage me to pursue the publication of my book.

I most gratefully thank the **Father, Son** and the **Holy Spirit** who is the author and finisher of my faith. To God be the Glory for flowing through me and speaking to me.

ACKNOWLEDGEMENTS

Thank you, **Bishop. Apostle. Rosa L. Williams** for pushing and putting the publication of this book into motion. I also want to thank all of my family who supported me, and all of my Everfaithful Missionary Baptist Church (EMBC) brothers and sisters in Christ.

I would like to thank the Almighty God who sits high and looks low, my big brother Jesus, and to the Holy Spirit, my tutor, and my guide. In me, is where he resides.

From The Heart of God
1st Corinthians 1:27-28

CHAPTER ONE: LOOK WHERE I BROUGHT YOU FROM

LOOK WHERE I BROUGHT YOU FROM

God said to me, *"Look! Look at where I have brought you from.*
Look at who you were and who you have become.
Once you were a little baby,
But now you have grown into a lady."

Once I heard God's voice
I realized that he was always strong when I was weak.
I said to God,
"Yes, it is true that I was hurt
Even after you picked me up out of the miry dirt
There were moments I still longed to sin
And live my past life again."

1st Corinthians 6:9-10,

Speaks of unrighteousness and I was one of every kind.

I lived in sin and unto righteousness, I was blind.

I accepted Christ at a young age

As the devil began to set the stage,

But God carried me as I was still his own.

And because of Calvary, I would never have to be alone.

I came to Christ at the age of six.

Not knowing what I was doing but wanting to be in the mix.

There came a time when I stopped going to church like I used to.

The devil did not want me to listen to God's Word.

The devil knew God's Word would heal my hurt,

And teach me my true worth.

As God's Word permeated, Jesus became my guide.

While the path was dim, his words were light.

He was always by my side.

He never walked away.

MY LOVE STORY

"Curiosity killed the cat is what you would say
Because you were so curious, you went astray.
When you were young, you sipped on some wine.
But your desires became stronger and grew with time.
You began using drugs when you were a teenager.
What you could not see was the reciprocity, the danger.
Drugs changed your appearance and brought twelve years of misery.
I am thankful that you came back to experience my grace and mercy.

You lost your husband, job, and home
But I never left you even when you felt most alone.
You were absent from your child
To feel free and run wild.
I let you run until you became tired.
The lower you fell, I was determined to lift you higher.
You were determined to do what you wanted to do,
And your sins were weights on you.

Gunshots were fired at you, and I spared your life.
In the midst of darkness, I continued to be your light.
Yes, I was there even when you neglected me
And your blinded eyes could not see.

I am the God of love, mercy, and grace.
No evil or principalities of this world can take my place.
I encouraged you to stop saying what you can and could not do.
Because you accepted me, the devil no longer had power over you.

I gave you back everything you lost.
I paid the cost.
I could have stayed up in glory
But you were a part of my story.

Your life was emptied and void.
I spoke life into existence, so you would not be destroyed.
I am the Lord.
Sadie, you are a good example.
Of all the reasons that I refuse to let go.

I reached way down in the pit you call bottomless,
Because you cried out, 'Lord, help me get out of this mess!'
You tell them that you could not stop on your own.
It is the Holy Spirit that convicts you of doing wrong.

The Holy Spirit makes you whole.
And sustains you from the evil that plans to permeate your soul.
While I reached for you to love me,
While I waited to give you the keys for victory,
And while I waited for you to be a part of my love story,
I longed to hear you say,
'Father, you are my heart's array
Father, I love you too.'

YIELD

Yield yourself to his rule.
Yield to his love.
Yield to his disciplinary rod.
Yield to his chastisement.

Remember, whomever he loves, he chastises.
Experiencing pain allows you to understand his love for you.
Oh yes! The devil will come after you.
Study the word and ask yourself, *"What would Jesus do?"*
Jesus was also tested with temptation.
The devil has no new tricks. He only has new faces.
There is nothing new under the sun.
Victory in Jesus is what you have already won.

The devil will seek to bring you down
He seeks to make you think negatively about yourself
He desires you to fail.
He will always strive to make you feel low.

The devil will place temptations before you
He will cause lies to appear to be true.
Satan will whisper lies that are not real
Affecting what you think and feel.

While Satan's tactics are false and weak
You have victory if Christ's face you seek.
If you believe,
You will receive.

Immerse yourself in the reading of God's Word.
Surround yourself in His grace
Which is sufficient to heal any past or present hurt.
Dwell in God's presence. He will give you peace all of your days.

YOUR WAITING WAS NOT IN VAIN

Based on Matthew 25: 1-13

The earth is one big waiting room.
God desires that none should perish.
We are like the bride waiting for the arrival of the bridegroom.
While we wait, remain without blemish.

Patiently wait
For Christ's return as he is like a bridegroom gone away
The moment will be sudden which he will appear
Awakening the dead in Christ
When we are least aware,
So let our oils remain and light burn.

While we wait, grow and learn
Our lamps should continue to burn
The Father will appear.
Arise and get prepared!
Arise and be ready!

Awake, those in sin.
Invite the Holy Spirit to come in.
Keep extra oil to burn
For you never know when the Master will return.

A WALK-THROUGH GOD'S GARDEN

One day, God walked through his garden.
He sought this particular person.
Elegance and majesty were his escorts.

God desired one thing which was the rose that occupied his mind.
He sought and did not retire to his courts
Until he found this rose so delicate and sweet.
On that day he chose the one he loves.
He saw a bud surrounded by thistles and thorns and said,
"I will pluck you up and let you live."

He touched her soul and placed the strength from above in her.
He gazed, amazed, as she bloomed
The word placed in her mouth gave life beyond the tomb.
She is blessed,
She is cherished.
He said,
"I have found another to do my will
Now you have grown into a beautiful flower,
Do not say you can't, or you do not have the knowledge.
I have given unto you the Holy Ghost inspired power."

The Father placed the rose in his hands.
He declared her life's plans
Saying,
"I chose you, Rosa!
You are the rose that fills my heart.
Although the path may become weary
Just plant the seed and I will be with you.
I'll do the watering,
And you will keep growing.

Rosa, I have given you the power.
To speak life during this hour.
I'm going to take you to another place for a reason.
Just keep on planting. The change will be in due season.

Never give up, do not give in.
I am separating the wheat from the tare.
Don't think all your seeds fell on bad ground.
Take a look Rosa-see who is still around.
I know everything, so have no regrets".

I ask each of you,
"By the show of hands out there, who has been blessed?"
Rev. Dr. Rosa L. Williams, be of good cheer!
God chose the right one.
God chose her.
Hear, Hear!
This is our prayer.
In only five words,
"Keep Rosa in every way."
Amen.

Oftentimes, we forget far too easily. Consider, thinking about how far God has brought you, and how he has helped you all the way through life's turmoil and pain. We often forget how God rescued us when we needed him the most. Although some moments, I was filled with weaknesses, God's grace was abundant in my bankruptcy of strength. I believed and trusted in Him with my whole heart for all He has done and for all He will do. God's love for us is beyond our understanding. For example, in moments when I was not closest to him, his love never ceased to manifest in my life. He drew me closer to me and showed me the way to righteousness. I poured out my heart to him, and he saw my sincerity. He taught me to fix my eyes on him and always trust in him.

Despite what you go through in life, always remember, and have faith! On earth, Jesus Christ was known for two things, his parables, and his miracles. Jesus shared a parable of the ten virgins. He explained how the virgins waited for the bridegroom to come for his wedding feast. The ten virgins had their lamps on, but they had waited for too long. Then, five of those women's oil ran low which caused their lamps to dim. When the bridegroom finally arrived, amongst the ten virgins, there were five who had extra oil while the last five, known as the foolish, were rejected because they were not present when the master arrived.

The five virgins who had extra oil were called the *wise virgins*, not because of their identity, rather it was due to their thinking ahead. They thought ahead and knew more oil would be needed even as the night grew dim. They were fully prepared for the coming of the Master, and their purchase of more oil showed their patience. Jesus told us to stay alert and wait for His coming. He is the bridegroom who will come soon, but we must be ready, so we do not be considered foolish. This places a responsibility on us to learn the art of managing our oil and not foolishly waste away the remaining time.

You may wonder, *"How can one waste the oil?"* For some, the allure of youthfulness leads them to various sins like lust and more. For others, it is a lack of integrity and strong character. Others burn their oil by remaining quarrelsome at all times, which can be utterly destructive to the image of Christ they may carry. The instruction that is implicit in this message is clear: To be among the wise virgins, you will have to make concrete decisions by choosing the way of Jesus anytime, anyplace, and anywhere. Trust me, there is always a pressure to sway from the path and go to places that are contrary to God's. However, I urge you to always hold on and keep believing. Like the famous hymnist said, *"Hold to God's unchanging hands."* Be among the wise virgins.

If you refuse to do your best, God may not bless the works of your hands. He knows you. He understands when you are putting in your best and when you are not. Lacking to give God your best makes it difficult for God's blessings to work in your life. The Bible teaches us that God will bless our work if our seeds are planted on good grounds. We do however have some points of weakness. Points when our strength just is not enough to propel us to achieving greatness. In those moments, God's strength is sufficient for us. We should always maintain this confidence that we can turn to God when we are very weak. God is the strongest fortress of peace, and the brightest beacon of hope when the days are darkest. As you turn to him during moments of weariness, look closely as he says, *"I will strengthen you, my child. Come and receive rest from me."* What great joy! We should remember that God has no respecter of persons, and he will never discriminate against anyone as people may do. To understand this better, we have to look through the acts of God in the scriptures. On various occasions, God lifted men and women of low estate into places of high esteem. For example, God did this to Saul, Moses, and one of the stories I love the most was that of Joseph's. In the case of Joseph, he had dreams of becoming great in life, yet his jealous brothers sold him into slavery. Looking through the eyes of men, everything seemed to be over for the young Joseph. Many would have advised him to calmly accept his circumstance and forget about any ever-achieving success in life. However, that is not what God said. God had plans for Joseph. Although the manifestation took time, it later came.

While Joseph blossomed in the house of Potiphar, he was falsely accused and thrown into a prison. At that point, it seemed as if destiny worked against Joseph. It would seem that his good luck charm had run out and his dreams become a thing of ridicule and of the past. God, however, made Joseph's story come out well. Through divine orchestration, Joseph was transferred into Pharaoh's palace and placed on a royal seat. God's plans were not finished. Through Joseph's wisdom and insights in governance, Egypt was able to preserve her food for the next seven years. Most importantly, God used Joseph to provide food and rest for his family and the rest of his tribe during a time of famine. What a great God!

I am very sure you still remember the story of David, the shepherd boy who was also forgotten by his father. While Jesse sent his other sons to attend to the noble profession of war in those days, he sent David to attend to sheep. At that point, many people would have written off David from ever accomplishing anything worth of note, talk less of becoming a king.

No one would have believed that David, the lowly shepherd boy, will go on to become a mighty king in Israel, the only King of Israel that never lost a battle. God glorified him by taking him from a job that took care of sheep to taking care of the people of Israelites. God constantly shows us throughout the scripture that he can do whatever he pleases with whom he pleases. Do you remember Esther? Do you remember her story? She was a slave in Israel. She never looked like a queen. However, she was a lady that obeyed and believed. God can take anyone from the dunghill to the palace. That is what he can do! He will do the same thing for you too. God absolutely loves you! You are his creation. He desires a relationship with you. That is all he desired from Adam in the Garden of Eden. God desires to have a relationship with the people he created. God made Adam, and gave him so much life, but only one warning, *don't eat of the forbidden fruit.* Disobedience set in and they did eat, causing them to lose the closeness of their relationship with the monotheistic God.

To this day, God desires that his people return to the place of communion that has been lost. Always remember the word according to Romans 6:23, *"The wages of sin is death, but the Gift of God is eternal life."* Hell was not initially made for you. It was meant for Satan and his demons. Do not treat God like a drive through restaurant, a quick convenience. God desires you to spend some time with him. For example, if a man desires to learn a skill, he will have to dedicate time to learn the skill. Whenever you want to learn from God and know his ways, you have to dedicate a large amount of time to knowing him.

Stay and fellowship more in the early hours of the morning and late at night. Spend quality time with him. Stay with him. We are his children. He yearns to teach you, his ways. He loves to show you the path of the righteous. Do not run far away from him.

Remember the prodigal son and how he ran far away from home? Your life would be terrible if you left the presence of God. Although you may enjoy the pleasures of sin for a while, your peace and joy would run out and people will desert you. Even in the lowest of moments, God is still there if you learn to pray to him.

God is mighty. His word is His power and when He speaks concerning an issue, consider it done because His word will never return void. God wants us to keep remembering that He is truth and can never lie. When he makes a promise, it stands till the end of time. We can believe in Him in every season of hurt. Though weeping and praying may tarry, God has got us in His hands. He promised to wipe the tears away from our face if we keep trusting Him for everything.

I am eternally grateful that God has shown me that the Kingdom of Heaven is most important. I am thankful that the Holy Spirit has taught me the importance of chasing God. I have come to the realization that when we begin to chase and follow God, many things we call important will not be most important.

CHAPTER TWO: I DID NOT ALWAYS KEEP MY EYES ON THE PRIZE

WISDOM

Based on Proverbs 4:7

You may ask, *"What is wisdom?*
Is it a gift from heaven?
Where does it come from?
Do we need it to build God's Kingdom?"

I say to you, *"Life will have trouble.*
If you want to overcome pray and stay humble.
Wisdom is something that we learn.
And it is something that we earn."

When the storm of life seems to rage
and we say a prayer or quote a sage.
That is wisdom in its tracks.
Keeping you pushing forward through life's setbacks
Wisdom is energy.
Enabling you to become who you are supposed to be.

Wisdom is will power.

That calls down God's Holy power

Which gives you an escape to victory

Whenever evil desires to destroy and defeat.

So yes, wisdom is the ability to make Godly choices.

Whenever you use wisdom, your soul rejoices.

It is a gift directly from heaven.

It is sent as a gift and a blessing.

Remember Your Creator While You Are Young
Poem based on Ecclesiastes 12:1

A lot of times when we are young
We are just having fun.
Enjoying everything and taking nothing in.
How many times is our youth spent in vain?

Like many others and maybe even you,
I was rebellious and lived in sin during my youth.
I lacked knowledge and failed to know the truth.
I encourage you to do things differently.
Show God that you are trustworthy.
Although it feels like a lifetime,
You are young only for only a short amount of time.

Know that at this stage in your life
Satan wants to blind you so that you never walk in the light
He will come into your heart and mind
Seeking to separate you from the True Vine
The True Vine is Jesus Christ
And he wants to shelter you in his light.

He loves you just the way you are
In a world of galaxies, you are his star!
Connect with your creator.
Acknowledge Him always for He is your maker.

Remember Your Creator While You Are Young

Get him on your mind.

Grow in grace with time.

For when the days of old has come

and life has gone down just like the sun.

It will be too late when the light of the sun, moon, and stars.

Grows dim to your old eyes.

You would look around and think, *"My youth is so far."*

It is then that you may realize.

That it was never too soon to give Christ your heart.

Let him in! Let him in!

Be a Christian, my friend.

Live this life so that you can live again.

We never know how or when.

Prepare your soul.

For one day you are young,

But if you live long

You will surely grow old.

WISDOM

———————◦———————

"But God has chosen the foolish things of this world to confound the wise; and has chosen the weak things of this world to confound the things which are mighty."
(1ˢᵗ Corinthians 1:27)

G od will take the foolish things of this world to confound the wise. His ways are far above our ways! His thoughts and patterns are far beyond ours! Because God's thoughts are so different from ours, one of the wisest things we can do is ask God for his wisdom. Because God loves us just as a good father loves his children, God is willing and able to endow us in his wisdom.

God's love was present in my life when I had no one else. His love never wavered through all of my trials and tribulations. God is there when you feel that you are all alone and no one cares. God is there when you have poured out and given more of yourself to others and do not reciprocate the same. Out of all the criticism, under mining, backstabbing, being used and abused, God was there! His love teaches wisdom.

Proverbs 4:7, *"Wisdom is the principal thing; therefore, get wisdom: and with all thy getting get understanding."* A man was once asked of which was greater between wisdom and strength and he replied that wisdom was greater. Solomon after making a great sacrifice to God at Gibeon was offered to ask for anything he wished for. Solomon had a choice of asking for anything in the world, and it would be granted at a moment's notice. However, he humbly admitted that he was young and clueless to the intricacies of leadership; therefore, he needed wisdom to lead the Israelites.

James 1:5 tells us that, *"If any of you lack wisdom, let him ask of God, that giveth to all men liberally, and upbraideth not; and it shall be given him."* God was impressed with Solomon's request and gave him wisdom that surpassed that of any man who lived before or after him adding wealth, power and glory to it. Solomon's request showed his humility before God admitting that he did not know what to do or how to lead. This wisdom was a divine wisdom that only comes from God. This is why he was the most powerful man in his days! Power and wealth may take you to the top, but without wisdom, you will not stay there.

God's Word has assured us giving us the boldness to ask wisdom of him just like Solomon did and He is ever ready to grant us this wisdom that we may live victorious lives here on earth. Despite how young or old we are, we can seek wisdom from the monotheistic God at any age. Ecclesiastes 12:1, *"Remember now thy Creator in the days of thy youth, while the evil days come not, nor the years draw nigh, when thou shalt say, I have no pleasure in them."* There were moments everything around me was suggesting that I give up and throw in the towel. However, I knew to seek God.

Just believe God! Having an understanding about God's compassion and how he shares wisdom, brought me to the point where I began to believe that God could help me. All I needed to do was to believe and trust in him! As simple as that sounds, all I needed to do was trust in God to allow him to deliver me from the fear and guilt I was always feeling.

I later realized that God is always with us in every step we take. He is always there even if we make bad decisions and get ourselves all wrapped up in our mess. God is always by our side waiting for us to run back to Him. He has always been there, from the first day you were born, and he will be there even till you take our final breath and come to meet with him. The questions that I would ask you are, *"Do we really know to communicate with God so that we can experience his compassion, love and wisdom? Do we really have that time to talk with him? Have you surrendered all that you have, and all that you are to him? Can we, while we live on earth give him a chance in our heart so he can help us through life."* Sadly, many do not, they just want to do what they want and never develop a relationship with God, but he is always patient, he is always waiting for us to come back to him.

The world we live in offers you a lot of distractions to cloud your vision and cheat out of what really matters- a life spent walking with God. Ecclesiastes teaches us to take heed and spend our youthful days seeking and serving God and not postpone the day of our salvation till later. In Psalms 90:10, 12, Moses says *"The days of our years are threescore years and ten; and if by reason of strength they be four-score years yet is their strength labor and sorrow; for it is soon cut off, and we fly away. So, teach us to number our days, that we may apply our hearts unto wisdom."* Life is like a dream that passes away quickly, much faster than anyone can take note of. The Bible says that the glory of the youth is their strength. Growing old is the natural order of things and cannot be broken or reversed. Wisdom is accepting that you cannot help yourself and asking for the help of the Savior by accepting His free gift of salvation. Then can you live out your youthful days in His service so that when you grow old, you would look back at the days of your strength and be grateful that they were wisely spent.

CHAPTER THREE: JESUS
PAID THE COST

PAID IN FULL

Poem Based On Romans 6:23

Burdened with the cost of sin.

As it read amounts that you could not afford to pay

Sin, shame, guilt, and humility

Would have left you broken and defeated.

If it was not for the price that Jesus paid

So that you would not have to be a slave.

It is a better day!

It is a better day

All because he came along,

And his love paved the way.

He paid my debt in full and covered me with his blood

Then he called me friend.

Now, I can live and live again

Because blood dripped

From his pierced hands.

I am born again.

KEEP IN MIND

Based on Psalm 139:14

You were made in God's image.

Just like Jesus, you are from David's lineage.

You are one of God's most beautiful flowers.

Always know that he will keep you every second of every minute,

And every minute of every hour.

You are special to him.

You are unique for his purpose.

You are the Apple of God's Eye.

He loves you so much!

God has His hands on you.

As long as you are pleasing to Him,

You will be blessed in whatever you do.

In him seek holiness and live.

Unto you, God will give, give, give.

God thinks thoughts of kindness towards you.

Regardless of the challenges you face,

You are not forgotten.

He will carry you through.

Keep the mind of Christ in you.

PAID IN FULL

Romans 6:23, *"For the wages of sin is death; but the gift of God is eternal life through Jesus Christ our Lord."* The world by means of Adam's sin fell under the power of the devil. Since then, sin multiplied throughout the earth and paved the way for death to reign on the earth. All life comes from God and man was a partaker of this life through constant fellowship with God. But when Adam disobeyed God's instructions, he was separated from God, who was his source. This explains why God warned him not to disobey. Genesis 2:16-17, *"And the LORD God commanded the man, saying, Of every tree of the garden thou mayest freely eat: But of the tree of the knowledge of good and evil, thou shalt not eat of it: for in the day that thou eatest thereof thou shalt surely die."* The story of the fall of man shows that this death meant separation of man from God which translated to death. Cut a branch from a tree and it dies. The same was the case of man and this separation is as a result of sin and the consequence of it is death. Death here does not just mean the physical cessation of life on earth but also an eternal separation of man from our Maker. It is manifest in the pain, sickness, and sorrows we see around us today.

The B part of Romans 6:23 shows that despite the damage that sin brought with it into the human race, God in His infinite mercies offer the gift of eternal life through Jesus Christ. John 3:16 says, *"For God so loved the world, that he gave his only begotten Son, that whosoever believeth in him should not perish, but have everlasting life."* Man sinned (breached the laws of God) and he got the consequence which was death. But God not wanting man to perish sent Jesus to Mankind. His mission was to save man from death (John 10:10 *The thief cometh not, but for to steal, and to kill, and to destroy I am come that they might have life, and that they might have it more abundantly.*) And ultimately reconnect man back to God which translates to eternal life.

We are hereby left with the choice of accepting this life which God offers freely in Christ Jesus or reject it and be held bound by the devil through sin leading to death. Psalms 139:14 states," *I will praise thee; for I am fearfully and wonderfully made: marvelous are thy works; and that my soul knoweth right well."*

Genesis 1:26-27 *And God said, Let us make man in our image, after our likeness: and let them have dominion over the fish of the sea, and over the fowl of the air, and over the cattle, and over all the earth, and over every creeping thing that creepeth upon the earth. So, God created man in his own image, in the image of God created he him; male and female created he them.* The above scriptures point out that you were made in God's image and likeness. When God made you, He made you to be like Him.

A lion cannot give birth to a goat, nor an eagle cannot hatch chicks from its eggs. Every form of life produces offspring of its own kind, light cannot produce darkness, it only produces light. This is a universal principle that can never be broken. The same goes with God. He made us that would function in his capacity here on earth. So quit thinking low of yourself because that is not who you are.

However, this truth is made a reality only in the life of those who has been reconnected to his source. The life that Christ offers us eternal life, the very life of God. This is the life that enables you to live and act like God does. Why not accept Him as your Lord and savior? Do not listen to the lies of the devil telling you that you are worthless and that your life does not count. It is all a lie. God has you in mind and that is why He sent Jesus to die for you and to restore you.

CHAPTER FOUR: HE MEANT
EVERY WORD

GOD SPOKE TO ME

Poem Based On Ecclesiastes 4:12

God truly knows your heart.
He spoke to me while we were distant and apart.
He said to me, *"You asked for this man and I gave him to you.*
It was my time and my choosing.

It was not by a chance or a sudden glance.
That you loved one another beyond your circumstance.
I knew you two,
And planted seeds as your love grew.
Now, I am taking him back!
He withstood the given task.

Yes, he was a good husband, father, grandfather, brother, and friend.
He wanted to be with you to the end!
I know that now tears fill your eyes.
But it was my grace that place you two in each other's lives.
Now, the process of him leaving is hard
You must cope, for this is the will of God."

Now I know,
It is never goodbye.
To the man I loved so;
Instead, it is, I will see you again up in God's sky!

IT IS ALREADY FINISHED

Poem Based On Isaiah 46:10

Why are we worried?
Our heads are often in the clouds of uncertainties.

Why do we over think things?
We often dwell on thoughts that are unnecessary.

Why do we worry?
When God has shown so many times how much he cares for you.

Believe.
On a cross, half dead and half alive
Jesus whispered, "It is finished!"
He every word.

HE MEANT EVERY WORD

The lilies are not worried about where they will get nutrients from or how well they are growing, yet they do not lack the right nutrients and are always beautiful. Even the Bible says that King Solomon in all his glory is not as beautiful as the lilies of the fields which the Lord takes care of. How much more you? You are not a plant, or an animal grazing in the fields but you are a child of God. You are God's child, and he loves you so much!

Isaiah 46:10A states, "*Declaring the end from the beginning, and from ancient times the things that are not yet done, saying, My counsel shall stand, and I will do all my pleasure;* "therefore, we know our story has already been written. God has not only planned but also numbered our days. Why worry about something God finished before the beginning of time? Why is your head filled with worries about tomorrow? God wants us to know that he has already mapped out our future. Do not worry about unnecessary things. The birds of the air do not worry about what they will eat or where they will lay their heads, yet God provides for them.

Because of Calvary, we are able to experience God's unmerited grace knowing that in all situations, he will take care of us.

When he hung his head while he was on that cross and said it was finished, it was not over; This was only the beginning. The beginning of a new life for all those who would look up and believe, a new path set out to reach God. It was the beginning of a new generation of people. After that time, Christianity would be born, and Christians would emerge as people whose hearts are interwoven with the ordinances of God. A true breed without greed, a set of people who would genuinely love God, people who have the love of God shared in their hearts, men and women of God who would walk in the footsteps of their savior Jesus Christ was birthed.

When Jesus said, *"It is finished,"* he meant it. He meant every single word of it. He meant that every pain that we feel, all our sicknesses and diseases are over! Every form of addiction is broken! We are no longer slaves to sin! We are no longer slaves to fear! We are children of God! The moment the statement, *"It is finished"* was uttered by Jesus, the veil covering the Holy of Holies in the temple was torn from top to bottom, this was a sign that God was saying that there is nothing that separates you and I anymore from the monotheistic God.

Jesus Christ died for the remission of sins. Jesus made us clean by His blood. Once we believe in him, we have access to God willingly knowing that God will never reject us. Isn't that amazing! Now God can speak, and a believer can hear clearly and respond to God. The Holy spirit now lives inside of us, so there is a confidence that we have, and we are so glad and happy that on that Jesus carried the John 1:12 states *"for as many that believe Him (Jesus), He gave power to become the sons of God."* If you believe in Jesus and in his sacrifice, you have automatically become a son of God. When Jesus said, *"It is finished."* That is not the end of the story. The story had just begun.

Do you believe that Jesus Christ is Lord? I encourage you today to make him a part of your story! Invite him into your life and ask him for the Holy Spirit. If you do this, God will renew and change your whole life. Trust him, and he will change you within your mind, heart, and spirit.

CHAPTER FIVE: ACCEPTING
WHAT GOD HAS ALLOWED

A SINCERE SERVANT

Poem Based On Romans 8:30

I find it to be a disturbance.

The way you desire to control my servant.

You are more concerned about your wants and not you needs.

Instead of desiring a servant who can lead.

You do not want a shepherd from the Lord.

You want someone who will sew in discord.

You do not want a man of God.

You want someone you can tell when to stop and start.

You do not want an anointed one.

You want to appoint one.

You do not want preacher of the Gospel.

You want someone to soothe your itching ears. You want a deceiver.

You do not want someone who believes in Christ.

You like bickering, and you fail to care about what is right.

You do not want someone to teach you about God's love, guidance,

and protection.

You want to give direction.

You do not want the truth.
You want the lies counterfeited as the truth.
You do not want to hear what you need.
You want to hear
Only what satisfies your ears.

You do not want a two-edged sword that cuts to the marrow.
You want to harden your heart like Pharaoh.
You would rather strife and division.
Than to build according to God's vision.

You would rather commit adultery, be fornicators, and have bad relations.
But you expect me to deliver you from trials and tribulations.
God is the truth.
He always knows what to do.
God did not raise a man of God to send here for you to do as you choose.
Read Route 66.
God does have the rules.
Can't you see what is happening?
Look around you.
The real people of God want to hear the truth.
Pastor is a great man of God. He is anointed, and he is a shepherd.
He is a preacher of the Gospel who God sent here to lead us.
So, get your mouth off of him.

It is not him you will have to deal with at the end.

It is God who you are actually fighting against.

The beginning and the end.

There is no way you are going to win.

God says,

"I have chosen him to fulfill His purpose.

Touch not my anointed, do my prophet no harm.

I am El-Shaddai-God Almighty and peace, El Shalom.

This is my house and until I say otherwise.

Pastor Jones is the spouse."

I AM IN THE RIGHT PLACE NOW

Poem Based On Psalm 26:8

Out of all the places that I have ever been.
For the first time ever, I enjoy each moment spent.
My life here and now is very blessed.
No cares, no pain, just experiencing God's promise.

I love where I am.
I love where I stand.
A place where I feel at home and at peace.
The place my heart has longed to never cease.
I am in the right place now.

God the Father is oh so awesome.
When my aunt died, I was never lonesome.
Jesus was here.
To console my fears
For the first time in my life, I realize the blessings of eternity.
Such as what it means to live and be free.

I love where I am.

I love where I stand.

A place where I feel at home and at peace.

The place my heart has longed to never cease.

I am in the right place now.

Jesus is everything; I no longer have to search.

His love permeates and floods my heart.

I am at the right place.

My heart now beats at the right frequency.

My mind is free

Because I have a newfound liberty.

My shoulders are now light because the burdens have been lifted.

Once I surrendered to Christ, my whole life shifted.

For a long time, I thought I would never find this place.

A place of happiness and calmness.

A place of love and grace.

Where I receive truth and righteousness.

ACCEPTING WHAT GOD HAS ALLOWED

H ave you ever wondered, *"Why does life have so many ups and downs? Why do things happen that we sometimes fail to understand?"* Romans 8:30, *"Moreover whom he did pre-destinate, them he also called: and whom he called, them he also justified: and whom he justified, them he also glorified."* The portion of scripture tells us that those whom God calls into His family are those He already predestined to be His children. And not just so, He justifies them so that they stand righteous (without fear or guilt) before Him and then eventually, He glorifies them. Do you now see why as a believer, you cannot live the way others do and talk the way they do? You have been called into the greatest family in the universe, the Kingdom of God. This in itself is the highest honor any man can attain.

Psalms 139:16-18 explains in further detail," *Thine eyes did see my substance yet being unperfect; and in thy book all my members were written, which in continuance were fashioned, when as yet there was none of them. How precious also are thy thoughts unto me, O God! how great is the sum of them! If I should count them, they are more in number than the sand: when I awake, I am still with thee."*

Long before you took your first breath, even before your parents were born, God knew you and planned your life! He sent His son, Jesus ahead of you to pave the way into His kingdom so that when you arrived, you would be able to fulfil the purpose for which He made you.

With the knowledge of this, lay to rest every worry that has before now plagued your heart and caused you so much anxiety. God has your life all planned out. You may wonder, *"What do I do if my life is all planned out by God?"* Psalms 40:7-8 gives a crystal-clear answer to this, *"Then said I, Lo, I come: in the volume of the book, it is written of me, I delight to do thy will, O my God: yea, thy law is within my heart."* Submit yourself to God. Fellowship with Him and He will direct you through His word on what He has planned out for you. It is more than you can ever imagine, trust me. You were made for so much more!

Psalms 26:8, *"LORD, I have loved the habitation of thy house, and the place where thine honor dwelleth."* Can you remember the first time you fell in love? Now let's relate this to our walk with God. If we say we love Him, then we must show it in our deeds, how we regard the things that concern Him and what He loves. If your spouse loves to cook, you may learn to love cooking also because of your love for them. The same applies to our love and walk with God.

Love is powerful! It is not powerful in words alone, but it is proven by actions. Actions, they say, speak louder than words. We cannot say we love God without loving what He loves. God loves His church. He loves the gathering of his children. I often feel so blessed to be in the place of worship where God has destined for me to be. I know that Bishop Rosa L. Williams has a mantle over her life, and the anointing God has given her has helped me to pull through so many of life's situations.

If you do not have a leader whose anointing breaks yokes, I encourage you to find one. Be in a place where you know your spirit will be uplifted once you attend worship if you are down and out. Psalms 133:1-3, *"Behold, how good and how pleasant it is for brethren to dwell together in unity!*

It is like the precious ointment upon the head, that ran down upon the beard, even Aaron's beard: that went down to the skirts of his garments.

As the dew of Hermon, and as the dew that descended upon the mountains of Zion: for there the LORD commanded the blessing, even life forevermore." Worship is designed by God to help his children get through hard times.

The scriptures above show us how important it is to God that His children come together in worship. This gathering of believers is where God dwells. It is therefore unchristian to not love it. Hebrews 10:25, *"Not forsaking the assembling of ourselves together, as the manner of some is; but exhorting one another: and so much the more, as ye see the day approaching."* I am as strong as I am today because I did not forsake to fellowship. I knew I needed to always attend church. Loving the house of God is an all-round beneficial experience for the believer. David said in Psalms 122:1, *"I was glad when they said unto me, Let us go into the house of the LORD."* I uplift my Bishop and I am eternally grateful to her and the zeal that God has placed upon her life. I am thankful for the Holy Spirit allowing me to know that I was and still am in the right place.

CHAPTER SIX: KEEP PRESSING ON

IF I TOLD YOU SO

Based On John 16:33

There are many of things that you do not know,

And their places you will never go.

The world is spinning fast.

Before you know it, the future will become the past.

Questions exist in your heart

About where to begin and where to end.

How can you prevent getting a late start?

How will you win when fighting against the wind?

No one wants to come in second place.

There were moments you longed for but could not feel my grace.

If I told you so,

Would you believe that I am still God,

The one who can make time start and stop?

If I explained that as God, I became a man.

I bore a cross, and pain penetrated my heart.

All that I was, people said I was not.

Just moments before I ascend.

I thought of promises made that would be fulfill

Before I again descend

I had no regrets; This my friend, was the Father's will.

Would you believe?

That I too, grieved?

Would you trust me still?

And stand in my will.

If I told you the way to victory

Is not all easy.

I wonder would you stay or would you go.

If I told you so.

A CHILD KILLED IN A CROSSFIRE

Based On 2nd Corinthians 5:8

I love you, mom.
I know life does not seem fair at times,
But I know I was the apple of your eye and your sunshine.

I apologize for being at the wrong place at the wrong time.
Leaning to my own understanding, caused me to cross that line.

A line I crossed
Which I wish I never did

I just wanted you to know you were good to me.
So do not let the devil or you cause you to feel guilty.
You see!

A line I crossed
Which I wish I never did.
We live in a world where you do not know when, where, or how.
But God was there. There is no doubt.

I love you, mom, and that is a fact.
So, take to Jesus arms.
He said He was coming back!!!

Love,
Jasmine

HAPPY MOTHER'S DAY MOM

I thank you for being you!

I thank you for the little things you do.

You have worried, you have cried.

You have stayed up all night.

You were happy and full of smiles

On the day I saw the light.

I know, I hurt you in the past years.

Lord knows,

I know you were full of tears.

Sometimes it seemed like veering your children was hard.

But mom, believe me you have done your part.

So, Mom, I pray for you.

Let go and let God.

Your love is so kind and true.

I love you, Mom.

I live for you.

Love Unconditionally,

Sadie

KEEP PRESSING ON

Philippians 3:14 *I press toward the mark for the prize of the high calling of God in Christ Jesus.*

Despite the many obstacles that we are challenged with, we should keep our hearts and minds focused on the prize, Jesus Christ. Life will have troubles and obstacles, but Jesus teaches us to be of good cheer because he has overcome the world. Of course, when we face devastations, we not only question God, but also, we search to find the Grace of God. We may even ask ourselves, *"Is this the will of God? Why me? Why my child?"* Sometimes trouble does not seem fair, but one thing for sure is that we will all face trouble at some point in our lives. Whenever I am faced with trouble, I often wonder, *"How to deal with this situation?"* This is a normal question. Although we will all encounter trouble in our lives, many times, we do not know how to respond to the trouble. I say to you, *"You may not understand your troubles, but respond to the circumstance with prayer."* Prayer, my friend, makes all of the difference. We have to pray to overcome!

John 16:33 states, *"These things I have spoken unto you, that in me ye might have peace. In the world ye shall have tribulation: but be of good cheer; I have overcome the world."* God did not promise us a life free of troubles! He did not promise us that each day would be easy, but the good news is that a safe landing is assured. No wonder David said in Psalms 23:4 *Yea, though I walk through the valley of the shadow of death, I will fear no evil: for thou art with me; thy rod and thy staff they comfort me.* David realized that on the earth, trials and obstacles are bound to occur to everyone. Even believers are not exempted. Our Lord Jesus went through the same and came out victorious. This is the confidence we have as children of God.

2nd Corinthians 5:8, *"We are confident, I say, and willing rather to be absent from the body, and to be present with the Lord."* Because of the troubles this world has to offer, we may yearn to be taken away to our place of eternal rest (heaven). This is understandable. No one wants to suffer pain. The fall of man in the Garden of Eden opened the door for Satan to infest God's beautiful earth with all manner of pain, sickness, and sorrow. Job 14:1, *"Man that is born of a woman is of few days, and full of trouble."* However, here are words comfort from the Savior: John 14:27, *"Peace I leave with you, my peace I give unto you: not as the world giveth, give I unto you. Let not your heart be troubled, neither let it be afraid."* Despite the troubles we face in this world, the peace of God shields our hearts from worry, and despair through faith and dependence on the promises of God.

How do we experience this peace that God gave us? Paul in his letter to the Philippians states it clearly in Philippians 4:6-8, *"Be careful for nothing; but in everything by prayer and supplication with thanksgiving let your requests be made known unto God. And the peace of God, which passeth all understanding, shall keep your hearts and minds through Christ Jesus. Finally, brethren, whatsoever things are true, whatsoever things are honest, whatsoever things are just, whatsoever things are pure, whatsoever things are lovely, whatsoever things are of good report; if there be any virtue, and if there be any praise, think on these things."* Keeping our minds on God's promises gives room for the peace of God to find expression in our lives. I encourage you to always seek the peace of God.

CHAPTER SEVEN: ANSWER WHEN GOD CALLS YOU

MY FATHER SENT ME

"For God sent not His son into the world to condemn the world; but that the world through him might be saved." (John 3:17)
From 40 +2 generations, I came. (Matthew 1:17)
God the Father, the Son and the Holy Spirit are all one
and the same. (1st John 5:7)
God stepped out in the flesh for His creation. (1st John 4:2)
Knowing all the mess it was in all their frustration.

I came so that you might have life and life more abundantly.
(John 10:10).
Bless you Father. Bless you indeed.
You sent me so that the captive would be free. (Luke 4:18)

We were just sitting there looking down on you.
Then the Father said, Son I have got something for you to do.
So, I obeyed Him and obeyed Him to the fullest
I prayed, *"Father, Father here am I"* (John 17:4).

I come to keep you from the sting of death
Because without me you would surely kill yourself (Hebrews 2:9).

I came to save the lost.

All you can think about is a price or what it will cost. (Mark 2:17)

I came to give life to the dead (Matthew 11).

You chose to do wrong instead (Romans 1:28, 32).

I came to be a mother and a father, even went like a sheep to the slaughter (Isaiah 53:7).

I came to open your eyes (John 9:15).

To let you know Satan is full of lies (John 8:44).

I came to tell you, "*I have everything you need and every meaning.*" (Philippians 4:19).

You still ask what the reason (Mark 2:8).

My Father has such a great love for you (John 3:16).

Yet you still reject the truth (John 14:5,6).

He offered you joy, and a peace of mind (John 14:27 & John 15:11).

You still are not ready, saying you have time (Mark 13:32).

His kindness you take for granted.

His goodness you just sit there and fan it (Romans 11:22).

His faithfulness will always be there (Matthew 28:30).

You do wrong without a care (Romans 1:32).

So, there I was sitting up in glory (John 3:12).

My Father said go Son and do this thing (John 17:18).

Cause without you nothing will change (John 3:17).

Knowing me the long- suffering I would have to endure (Isaiah 52:53).

He sent me because the world needed a cure (Isaiah 53:12).

Now, I stand at the door and knock (Revelation 3:20).

You have the nerve to have a vacancy sign which is a block (John 12:40; Mark 6:52).

I died on the cross (Matthew 27:32-35).

Only to rise in three days (John 2:19).

God is the boss (Genesis 1).

I chose you. You did not choose me (John 15:16).

I did not have to do it. Don't you see.

My yoke is easy.

My burden is light (Matthew 11:29-30).

Walk with me.

I will fight your fight (2nd Chronicles 20:15).

Yes, I am alive and well.

If you keep rejecting me,

You will spend in eternity in Hell (Matthew 23:13; Luke 12:5; Psalm 55:15).

What I have for you is to gain.

It is not a loss (Philippians 1:21)

But I will not force Salvation on you.

It is your choice (2nd Chronicles 2:5).

You may seek me now.

Who knows when the time will come?

When I cannot be found (John 7:36; Psalm 32:6; Isaiah 56:6).

Bend your legs. Get down on your knees.

Say, *"Here Am I Lord. Do as you please."*

If you do not have legs, do not worry about that.

I will come to you right where you are.

You see, I rose from the grave with all powers. I am the Lilly of the Valley. I am the real flower.

Get in touch with me as soon as you can. Who am I? My name is Jesus! (John 19:5; Mark 14:62).

ANSWER WHEN GOD CALLS YOU

The world was held under the lordship of the devil from the very moment Adam and Eve disobeyed God in the Garden of Eden. When Christ came, he did not only wash away man's sin, but also, he took away the nature of sin that separated man from God. Hallelujah, praise God for his son Jesus the Christ! John 3:16, *"For God so loved the world, that he gave his only begotten Son, that whosoever believeth in him should not perish, but have everlasting life."* Knowing that we can now live to live again is a blessing, and we should eternally be thankful unto God.

Salvation is a gift God gave to mankind. An important feature of a gift is that it is not worked for, but it is freely given. However, a gift can either be accepted or rejected. John 3:18, *"He that believeth on him is not condemned: but he that believeth not is condemned already, because he hath not believed in the name of the only begotten Son of God."* To accept this gift of God is to believe in Jesus and what He came to do for us. To reject it is to doubt what he did for us.

My beloved friend, the scripture is clear, so you have a choice to either be free from the power of the devil and come into the family of God by accepting the free gift of salvation that God has offered you on the platter of grace or reject it by not believing in Jesus and by doing so, choose death. As mentioned, God gives you a choice. Will you choose to live the life that God has planned for you, or will you neglect God, his voice, his guidance, and his plans for your life?

Did you know that the choice is yours to make? Deuteronomy 30:19," I *call heaven and earth to record this day against you, that I have set before you life and death, blessing and cursing: therefore, choose life, that both thou and thy seed may live."* If you choose to allow God to come into your heart, he will teach you his will for your life.

CHAPTER EIGHT: FROM MY HEART TO PAPER

FOR COVID 19

We are here to serve others as well as ourselves.
Taking care of the sick, homeless, the wayward, and everyone else.
We are encouraged with our words.
We should be swift to be listeners,
And not abruptly speaking or just wanting to be heard.

We are all here for a very good reason.
Not to bring the company down, certainly not to commit treason.
Some of us are fast and some are slow.
Your pace is an important part of it.
But our major concern is keeping down bacteria growth.

We are people of integrity, collaboration,
accountability, professional development, and leadership.
We will not go against our values or flip the script.

We are people of high standards,
High values, and consistent standards.
We will not lean over to go against our standards or values.

We are all on a big ship and want to keep it afloat.
Cause if the captain goes down, we all are going to
need a raft or boat.
So, let's be real and do our very best.
Because sooner or later we will be out of this test.

IN THE BEGINNING, GOD HAD A PLAN

Before we were born,
Crafted by clay and placed in our mother's womb
God had a plan.

Before the sun was high in the sky
Or the moon shone its dim light,
God had a plan.

Before the day and night
Or before days were placed in calendars,
God had a plan.

Before Eve ate the fruit
Or before the serpent ate the dust,
God had a plan.

God had a plan
Mapped out, etched by His signature
A plan that predates back to existence
A plan to liberate and help humankind.

A PLAN, SO BEAUTIFUL

When we think about the Grace of God, it is truly a beautiful story. Romans 5:6-8, *"For when we were yet without strength, in due time Christ died for the ungodly. For scarcely for a righteous man will one die: yet peradventure for a good man some would even dare to die. But God commendeth his love toward us, in that, while we were yet sinners, Christ died for us."* Everyone did not like or love Jesus. People still challenged him and even Satan tried to tempt him to bow to him, but Jesus refused and kept His eyes on the prize. While speaking to people and preaching, a sect of religious leaders always found a way of always questioning what He did and asked questions to find fault but of course they never succeeded.

Acts 10:38, *"How God anointed Jesus of Nazareth with the Holy Ghost and with power: who went about doing good and healing all that were oppressed of the devil; for God was with him.* Jesus was healing and teaching throughout the land. Everywhere he went, he always performed miracles and taught the people. He became known for doing the impossible, like giving sight to a blind man, healing the lame and raising the dead back to life. The miracles of Jesus were so marveling, and this made a lot of people believe and follow him. He had a large crowd with him on the mountain and after teaching them, he decided to feed them, but His disciples had so little. A small boy in the crowd gave Jesus five loaves of bread and two fishes. Jesus took it and performed an amazing miracle of sharing it among five thousand people. That was indeed marveling!

Just like some of us today are scared of what we do not understand. It was all a part of God's plan for Jesus to be rejected. They stripped Him and put Him on a scarlet robe. They placed a crown of thorns and put it on His head. Then they mocked Him, these are the words they said. *Hail king of the Jews.* After all the spitting and all the mocking, they took off the cloak and put His own garments back on. Do you really understand what He went through for us, He is God's right-hand man He could have stayed on the throne? They led Him away bearing a cross. To a place called Golgotha, for a dying world that had no idea that they were lost. They gave Him vinegar to drink. Another cruel act, don't you think? They parted His garments amongst them. Casting lots of underneath Him. He was being ridiculed all over again. By the same very people on that cross. He carried our sins!

This is a God call, God is calling us to see what He is seeing, He is calling us up to believe what His son did on that cross on calvary. After going through all that pain for you and for me, He wants us to believe His works and live free of condemnation and of guilt. He has paid the price, then there is no need paying any other price for your sin. No price is higher than the price that Jesus paid on that cross of calvary. He shed His blood and died in place of you and me. All that is left for us is to believe and walk in that understanding that He has done it for us. That understanding gives us the strength to stand out amidst the crowd of people walking in sin, an understanding that Christ has paid for your sins will always make you happy.

A good analogy, I usually give is that imagine you went to a store to buy some items and when you were done picking the items you wanted, you then proceeded to the cashier to pay for the items you had bought, after waiting in line for your turn, you place your hand into your purse to get out your credit card and then you figure out that the credit card is not in your purse. It seems you may have forgotten your card home, just when you were in the middle of your thoughts the cashier says "That will be $37.45 ma'am, Card or cash?" You finally look up and you have neither, the crowd behind you is getting impatient and just then, someone tells the cashier, "don't worry, I got it." Signaling that you can go with the items you bought but you never spent a dime on any of the items.

Isn't that amazing. To think that you got those items without spending your money and you never expected that person to have paid for you. That's what Jesus did. We wouldn't have been able to pay for our sins even if you went home to get our credit card. We could not have been able to meet up to God's standard for staying pure and not committing sin but Jesus' death on the cross is proof that it is possible, very possible. Jesus paid the price and all we need to do is to believe in this sacrifice.

Another really interesting analogy is a person who had just committed murder, he knows that the Judge will rule him as guilty and he will be sentenced to death. He waits for his death and then when the Judge is about to declare her judgement someone stands in the court and say, "*Let him go, sentence me to death in his place, let me pay the price.*" Can you imagine how the face of the murderer will look like. He will be dumbfounded and when he leaves that place, he lives as a free man because someone has already paid for his sins.

You may have run away for too long. Well, it is never too late to take come back to God and ask Him for mercy. He has paid the ultimate price for you then there is basically no need for you to suffer and pay those prices for the sin, you will have to accept His sacrifices. This is why that all we owe God is to honor him and serve him, we have to be faithful to Him in all we do. We have to give Him honor all the time, for the love He has showered on us for dying on that cross for our sins and paying the ultimate sacrifice. It is God's love and dedication towards me that has made me make the vow *for God I live for God I die*. I have decided to serve Him! Because He first loved me, I love him even more!

1 John 4:19 *We love him, because he first loved us.*
For God I live for God I die...

CHAPTER NINE: THERE'S A MESSAGE IN MY REST

THERE'S A MESSAGE IN MY REST

Poem Based On John 13:34

Love one another, be kind to one another.
Always stay in touch.
You never know when a person needs to talk,
Say I love you or just maybe had enough.

Life, they say is short.
Too short for you to take things too personal.
Learn to forgive, let go of hate.
Learn to accommodate people.

Show kindness to those who feel they do not deserve it.
Smile, smile at them, make them laugh.
Always encourage them when they feel weak.
Say, "*I love you!*" They may just want to hear it.

Life is good to live.
But it's up to you to be in the fast lane or to just be still.
You see love comes in all shapes, forms, and fashion.
But the one to really count is your actions.

Life, they say is short.
Too short for you to take things too personal.

Learn to forgive, let go of hate.
Learn to accommodate people.

Everyone makes mistakes.
No one is perfect but you can become better.
Never write anyone off
Learn to always encourage.

I love you all! Do not forget that!
I know this is not the end and that is a fact.
Jesus Christ's love for our life. He sacrificed.
He is the one that paid the price.
Life, they say is short.
Too short for you to take things too personal.
Learn to forgive, let go of hate.
Learn to accommodate people.

So, to all of you I say,
"Pull together, say and love each other every day.
Oh! And when you think of me. Think of my smile.
That should brighten your day for a while.

Life, they say is short.
Too short for you to take things too personal.
Learn to forgive, let go of hate.
Learn to accommodate people."

THE LORD WILL BRING YOU BACK

Poem Based On Hebrews 7:25

You wonder, you plunder sometimes listening to your own
Mind will put you under.
Me, being selfish and catering to my flesh.
Entrapped by my own boldly lust. When I already knew better.
My own thoughts said it did not matter.

So, I fell again, again, and again.
Just like Israel, I stayed in sin.
God's Word is the truth there is nothing new under the sun.
Every battle you are faced with He has already won.

I remained a slave to sin's lustful appetites.
I fell but I stood, I fell again and stood.
For how long I will keep falling
The Bible says the righteous will stand after every fall.

I have believed that and stayed with God.
He has trusted and believed in me.
He loves me and has always given me an opportunity for growth.

Everything happens for a reason.

So, me and with my hard head had to go out and commit treason.

God brought me to this beautiful place.

My heart was at ease and I felt so safe.

He put me with a family that showed powerful love.

Such caring and support I knew it had to be from above.

On this rock He built His church.

A secure Godly foundation, boy was I a jerk.

I left running and somewhat having an excuse.

Leaning to my own understanding is what put me on the loose.

God was here and I knew that to be true.

So why would I leave where He was to go someplace new.

My life took a turn when I went away.

When God put you somewhere it is best to stay.

knew I had not only hurt myself.

I sinned against God and made a bad impact on everyone else.

It took a minute for me to make up my mind once more.

It finally happened the morning of September 2009.

I was so sorrowful for what I had done.

God had not given up on me. He saw the blood of His Son.

You see Everfaithful the day that I left.

It was you in heart I always felt.

You are like a strong Tower.

When I'm here I can see and feel God's power.

The shepherd that God has placed over you.

Bishop Williams, you are truly worthy of the honor that is due.

And the elders who are on her left and right

Are following her as she follows Christ.

I am destined to be in this place.

I am back and it is by God's grace.

So Ever faithful happy anniversary to you

It was the word of God that was taught and brought me through.

THERE'S A MESSAGE IN MY REST

J ohn 13:34 *A new commandment I give unto you, That ye love one another; as I have loved you, that ye also love one another.* If there was no love in the earth, life would have been meaningless. Love is what made God create man and even when man fell, love made God seek him out and send Jesus down to earth to save him from eternal death.

Matthew 5:13-16 puts it clearly this way, "Ye *are the salt of the earth: but if the salt has lost his savor, wherewith shall it be salted? It is thenceforth good for nothing, but to be cast out, and to be trodden under foot of men. Ye are the light of the world. A city that is set on a hill cannot be hidden. Neither do men light a candle, and put it under a bushel, but on a candlestick; and it giveth light unto all that are in the house. Let your light so shine before men, that they may see your good works, and glorify your Father which is in heaven."* From the scripture verses above, we see that believers are reminded of their nature as children of God. God is love, and His sons and daughters ought to exhibit this same nature. This love is the salt and light that Jesus was speaking of in John 13:34. When a man dwells in love, he automatically dwells in God because God is love. It is his very nature.

It is this love that saves men by drawing them to the gospel of the kingdom. Like a flame in the dark, love is the light that illuminates our dark world, and no man can resist light in the midst of darkness. Matthew 22:37-40, *Jesus said unto him, Thou shalt love the Lord thy God with all thy heart, and with all thy soul, and with all thy mind. This is the first and great commandment. And the second is like unto it, Thou shalt love thy neighbor as thyself. On these two commandments hang all the law and the prophets. "* If we say we love God, then we have no option but to also love our fellow men as this is the ultimate proof of our love for God.

Do you feel like you have strayed too far from the course of life that God planned out for you? Hebrews 7:25, *"Wherefore he is able also to save them to the uttermost that come unto God by him, seeing he ever liveth to make intercession for them. "* Jesus is calling to you. It is no mistake that your eyes are going through these words. It was the Father's working that you should come across this and yield your heart to Him.

John 6:37, *"All that the Father giveth me shall come to me; and him that cometh to me I will in no wise cast out. "* This scripture lays to rest every fear of being condemned or rejected by God when we come to Him. He is love and love does not condemn. He stands at the door of your heart, knocking. It is time to open up to Him.

The devil may have been telling you that it's too late for you, that God cannot forgive you. That is not so! Luke 23:42-43, *"And he said unto Jesus, Lord, remember me when thou comest into thy kingdom. And Jesus said unto him, Verily I say unto thee, To day shalt thou be with me in paradise. "* The repentant thief gained forgiveness and eternal life on the cross because he believed in Jesus and that was the turning point in his life.

Jesus is calling out to you today! Will you open the door for Him to come in and turn your life around? Hebrews 7:25, "*The anchor scripture of this text spells it out plainly that God is able to save you completely from whatever mess you may have gotten yourself into.*" It is not too late for you as long as you are still breathing. The Father is calling for you to come home.

CHAPTER TEN: YOUR STUFF IS ALREADY PAID FOR

YOUR STUFF IS ALREADY PAID FOR

Poem Based On Isaiah 53:1-12

From a little bitty baby, lying in a manger wrapped
In swaddling clothes.

He grew up as a carpenter, preached the Gospel was sold
For 30 pieces of gold.

Picked out in a line up with a simple kiss handled roughly
While not even trying to resist.

Went on to court for telling the truth.

He had no intentions of defending Himself
Not even a dispute
But, he was judged and sentenced to death,
By the same very people
He came to help.

They chose a murderer over Him,
Condemning the wrong man was their kill.

Christ was spat on and whiped. They made a mockery of Him.

He could have called for help, but He did not give in

He was disfigured and so very scared.

But the bruises did not stop Him – you see He was on a mission from God.

So, He went on to the top of Golgotha Hill

Carrying that heavy cross that man had built.

They nailed Him in His hands, they nailed Him in his feet, they pierced Him in His side, maybe just for an extra treat.

He was buried in a borrowed tomb guarded by guards.

He was not there. Jesus was busy tying up the loose ends for our new start.

He went to the grave, took the sting out of death, and made them behave. Then he went to hell to have a one on one with Satan to let Him know that death tried to take Him as a child.

But our big brother Jesus had a powerful anointing on His life.

Oh, the pain He suffered for you and me.
A king He is and a king he'll forever be.

You see He loves us so much.

That He took on all of our stuff! Remember: when Jesus was on that cross. He took on all our iniquities all our transgressions

All He asks is that we believe in Him with a confession.

NOTES TO THE VETERANS

I salute you!

You are the ones who have been in combat.

Some of you did and some of you did not come back.

You are the ones who fought battles not just for yourselves, but for me and everyone else.

You are the ones who were sometimes drafted

And what you wanted did not always matter.

You are the one who even signed up maybe to better yourselves but still you took part of the bitter cup.

You are the ones who had to be trained from a civilian to become a professional.

You have had all kinds of training and skills getting equipped to know how to live.

You have had duties for a long period of hours.

While I was safe at home watching television of taking a shower,

You were jumping out of aircrafts in foreign land.

Getting in position to make a standby water, ocean and sea.

Any means necessary to keep me free.

You are the ones who were trying to make peace-

While I was at home in bed getting my sleep.

You are the ones who sometimes lost body limbs or even your sanity

Even after that you did not think it was vanity.

You are the ones who left your family and homes praying to God to

keep both of you strong. So, the Air Guard, National Guard, Army,

Navy Airforce and Marines.

What you did for me still remains to be seen.

I just want you to know that I appreciate and salute all of you for

only God knows you what you have been through.

Freedom is not free.

Someone is always paying the price for you.

YOUR STUFF IS ALREADY PAID FOR

saiah 53:4-7, *"Surely he hath borne our griefs, and carried our sorrows: yet we did esteem him stricken, smitten of God, and afflicted.*

But he was wounded for our transgressions, he was bruised for our iniquities: the chastisement of our peace was upon him; and with his stripes we are healed.

All we like sheep have gone astray; we have turned everyone to his own way; and the LORD hath laid on him the iniquity of us all.

He was oppressed, and he was afflicted, yet he opened not his mouth: he is brought as a lamb to the slaughter, and as a sheep before her shearers is dumb, so he openeth not his mouth."

Have you ever sat down to wonder, *"What did it cost God to save you from the shackles of sin?" What He went through to deliver you from the kingdom of darkness into the marvelous kingdom of Christ Jesus, the dominion of the devil into the liberty in the family of God?"* The scriptures above provide a glimpse of what Jesus went through to save you and I.

The divine law is clear in Hebrews 9:22, *"And almost all things are by the law purged with blood; and without shedding of blood is no remission."* God saw that man was helpless, and He did what only He could do. He gave Himself in the person of Jesus to save us from our hopeless situation. The blood of man was tainted with sin; therefore, could not be accepted as a sacrifice for man. The only one who could save man was God and He did just that.

God shed His blood to satisfy the demands of divine justice. He took away the very nature of sin and nailed it to the cross and restored us. Colossians 2:14-15, *"Blotting out the handwriting of ordinances that was against us, which was contrary to us, and took it out of the way, nailing it to his cross; And having spoiled principalities and powers, he made a shew of them openly, triumphing over them in it."* Beloved, it cost Christ His own life to save you from death. An immortal dying for a mortal. That is how much God loves us! We are no longer debtors, but free to live and please Him all our days. Aren't you glad that Jesus Christ paid it all?

Made in the USA
Columbia, SC
28 May 2021

38698056R00059